PRINCEWILL LAGANG

Global Business in the 21st Century:
Entrepreneurial Strategies

First published by PRINCEWILL LAGANG 2023

Copyright © 2023 by Princewill Lagang

All rights reserved. No part of this publication may be reproduced, stored or transmitted in any form or by any means, electronic, mechanical, photocopying, recording, scanning, or otherwise without written permission from the publisher. It is illegal to copy this book, post it to a website, or distribute it by any other means without permission.

Princewill Lagang asserts the moral right to be identified as the author of this work.

First edition

This book was professionally typeset on Reedsy.
Find out more at reedsy.com

Contents

1. Global Business in the 21st Century: Entrepreneurial... 1
2. Global Market Research and Analysis: Uncovering... 4
3. Global Strategic Planning: Navigating Complexity 8
4. Global Market Entry and Expansion: Execution and Growth... 12
5. International Marketing and Global Brand Development 16
6. Global Sales and Customer Service Excellence 20
7. Global Operations and Supply Chain Management 24
8. Global Finance and International Expansion Strategies 28
9. Innovation and Sustainability in the Global Marketplace 32
10. The Future of Global Business: Trends and Projections 36
11. Strategic Leadership in Global Business 40
12. Global Business Ethics and Responsible Citizenship 44

1

Global Business in the 21st Century: Entrepreneurial Strategies

Introduction

In the fast-paced and interconnected world of the 21st century, global business has undergone a profound transformation. Entrepreneurial strategies have become central to navigating the complex landscape of international commerce. The convergence of technology, globalization, and shifting market dynamics has created both unprecedented opportunities and challenges for businesses. This chapter provides an in-depth exploration of these changes and the strategies that entrepreneurs must embrace to thrive in this dynamic global environment.

1.1 The New Global Landscape

The 21st century has ushered in a global business landscape that is more interconnected than ever before. The barriers to entry for international markets have significantly lowered, enabling businesses of all sizes to participate in global trade. Advances in technology, communication, and logistics have made it easier to reach customers worldwide. However, this interconnectedness has also exposed businesses to greater competition, volatility, and regulatory complexity.

1.2 The Rise of Entrepreneurial Strategies

Entrepreneurial strategies have become indispensable in this new era of global business. Entrepreneurs are no longer limited to startups and small enterprises; even established corporations are increasingly adopting entrepreneurial mindsets to stay agile and innovative. The ability to identify and capitalize on emerging opportunities, while mitigating risks, has become a critical skill for all business leaders.

1.3 Key Themes in This Chapter

This chapter will explore several key themes that underpin the dynamic nature of global business in the 21st century:

1.3.1. Technological Innovation

The rapid pace of technological innovation has revolutionized the way businesses operate. The chapter will delve into how emerging technologies, such as artificial intelligence, blockchain, and the Internet of Things, are transforming industries and creating new possibilities for entrepreneurial ventures.

1.3.2. Globalization and Supply Chains

Globalization has extended the reach of businesses into new markets, but it has also made supply chains more complex and vulnerable. This section will discuss how entrepreneurs navigate the global supply chain landscape, including strategies for risk management, diversification, and sustainability.

1.3.3. Market Disruption

Market disruption is a constant in the 21st-century global business environment. The chapter will highlight examples of disruptive innovations and examine how entrepreneurs can adapt to, and even instigate, market disruptions.

1.3.4. Entrepreneurial Mindset and Leadership

Entrepreneurial success is not solely determined by business plans and strategies but also by leadership and the mindset of the individuals driving the venture. This section will explore the characteristics and skills that define successful entrepreneurial leaders.

1.4 Structure of the Chapter

The chapter is divided into several sections, each focused on one of the key themes mentioned earlier. Each section will include real-world case studies, expert interviews, and practical insights to provide a comprehensive understanding of entrepreneurial strategies in the 21st-century global business context.

1.5 Conclusion

The global business landscape is evolving at an unprecedented rate, creating both opportunities and challenges for entrepreneurs. In this chapter, we will delve into the intricacies of global business in the 21st century and the entrepreneurial strategies that are essential for success. By the end of this chapter, readers will have a solid foundation for navigating the complex, ever-changing world of international commerce.

2

Global Market Research and Analysis: Uncovering Opportunities

Introduction

Chapter 2 explores the critical role of market research and analysis in the 21st-century global business landscape. In a world where markets are constantly evolving, and customer preferences are fluid, effective market research is the foundation of informed decision-making and entrepreneurial success.

2.1 The Importance of Market Research

This section highlights the central role of market research and why it's essential for businesses looking to operate on a global scale. It covers the following key points:

- Understanding market dynamics
    - Identifying customer needs and preferences
    - Assessing competition

- Mitigating risks

2.2 The Global Market Research Process

This part of the chapter outlines a structured approach to global market research. It includes the following steps:

2.2.1 Defining Research Objectives

- Clearly stating what you aim to achieve with your research
    - Setting specific goals for data collection and analysis

2.2.2 Data Collection

- Different methods of data collection (surveys, interviews, secondary data sources)
    - The role of technology in data collection

2.2.3 Data Analysis

- Quantitative and qualitative data analysis
    - Tools and techniques for meaningful insights

2.2.4 Market Segmentation

- How to divide your target market into meaningful segments
    - Tailoring your approach to different segments

2.3 Global Market Trends and Emerging Markets

This section focuses on the importance of staying up-to-date with global market trends and explores the potential of emerging markets. It includes:

- How to monitor and interpret trends
    - The challenges and opportunities in emerging markets
    - Case studies of successful businesses capitalizing on trends and emerging markets

2.4 Market Entry Strategies

Once you've conducted market research and identified opportunities, you need to decide how to enter these markets. This section discusses various market entry strategies, including:

- Exporting and importing
    - Licensing and franchising
    - Joint ventures and strategic alliances
    - Foreign direct investment

2.5 Competitive Analysis

Understanding your competitors is crucial in global business. This part of the chapter covers:

- Analyzing the strengths and weaknesses of competitors
    - Assessing market positioning
    - Strategies to gain a competitive edge

2.6 Ethical Considerations in Global Market Research

Market research must be conducted ethically and responsibly. This section addresses:

- Privacy concerns and data protection
    - Cultural sensitivity in global research
    - Ethical considerations when entering new markets

2.7 Conclusion

Chapter 2 underscores the significance of global market research and analysis in uncovering opportunities and making informed decisions in a rapidly changing global business environment. By following the principles and processes outlined in this chapter, entrepreneurs are better equipped to navigate the intricacies of international markets. The chapter sets the stage for subsequent discussions on strategic planning and implementation in the global arena.

3

Global Strategic Planning: Navigating Complexity

Introduction

Chapter 3 delves into the intricacies of global strategic planning. In the dynamic 21st-century business environment, effective strategic planning is the linchpin of success. This chapter explores how entrepreneurs can formulate and implement strategies to thrive in a global landscape rife with complexity and uncertainty.

3.1 Understanding the Global Business Environment

This section provides an overview of the global business environment and its complexities. Key points include:

- The impact of geopolitical factors
    - Socio-cultural considerations
    - Economic trends and trade policies
    - Technological disruptions

3.2 The Strategic Planning Process

This part of the chapter introduces the process of global strategic planning. It includes:

3.2.1 Setting Objectives

- Clearly defining short-term and long-term objectives
    - Aligning objectives with the company's mission and vision

3.2.2 Environmental Analysis

- SWOT analysis: Identifying strengths, weaknesses, opportunities, and threats
    - PESTEL analysis: Evaluating political, economic, social, technological, environmental, and legal factors

3.2.3 Strategy Formulation

- Developing strategic alternatives
    - Evaluating and selecting the most suitable strategies

3.2.4 Strategy Implementation

- Aligning resources and actions with the chosen strategy
    - Assigning responsibilities and establishing performance metrics

3.2.5 Strategy Monitoring and Adaptation

- Ongoing evaluation of strategy effectiveness
    - Making adjustments in response to changing circumstances

3.3 Risk Management in Global Strategy

Global business is inherently risky, and this section discusses:

- Identifying and assessing risks in international markets
    - Strategies for risk mitigation and contingency planning
    - Case studies on successful risk management in global operations

3.4 Global Strategic Alliances and Partnerships

Collaboration is often a key element of global success. This part of the chapter covers:

- Types of strategic alliances (e.g., joint ventures, partnerships)
    - How to identify suitable partners
    - Best practices for managing global collaborations

3.5 Corporate Social Responsibility (CSR) in Global Strategy

Ethical considerations and corporate social responsibility are integral to modern global business. This section discusses:

- The importance of CSR in global strategy
    - Implementing socially responsible practices
    - The impact of CSR on brand reputation and sustainability

3.6 Case Studies and Practical Insights

Throughout the chapter, real-world case studies and expert interviews provide practical insights into global strategic planning. Examples include businesses that successfully adapted their strategies in response to market disruptions and geopolitical shifts.

3.7 Conclusion

Chapter 3 underscores the importance of strategic planning in the global business context. It emphasizes the need for adaptability and a thorough understanding of the complexities and risks associated with international markets. Entrepreneurs who master the principles of global strategic planning are better equipped to navigate the challenges and seize the opportunities presented by the 21st-century global landscape. This chapter sets the stage for further discussions on the execution of strategies in diverse international markets.

4

Global Market Entry and Expansion: Execution and Growth Strategies

Introduction

Chapter 4 explores the practical aspects of entering and expanding in international markets. While strategic planning sets the course, execution and growth strategies determine the success of global ventures. This chapter provides insights into the operational, logistical, and marketing aspects of global market entry and expansion.

4.1 Market Entry Strategies Revisited

This section revisits market entry strategies and focuses on the practical aspects of each approach. It includes:

- Practical steps for exporting and importing
  - Licensing and franchising agreements
  - Key considerations for joint ventures and alliances
  - Challenges and benefits of foreign direct investment

4.2 Tailoring Products and Services for Global Markets

Global markets are diverse, and customization is often key. This section discusses:

- Product and service adaptation for local markets
    - The role of cultural sensitivity in product design
    - Strategies for maintaining quality while meeting local demands

4.3 Pricing and Marketing Strategies

Pricing and marketing strategies often need adaptation for global markets. Key points include:

- Currency fluctuations and pricing decisions
    - Localization of marketing campaigns
    - The role of digital marketing and social media in global promotion

4.4 Distribution and Supply Chain Management

Effective distribution and supply chain management are vital for global success. This section covers:

- Strategies for efficient global distribution
    - The role of e-commerce and logistics in international supply chains
    - Risk management in supply chain operations

4.5 Regulatory Compliance and Legal Considerations

Navigating international regulations and legal considerations is essential. This part of the chapter discusses:

- Compliance with local laws and regulations

- Intellectual property protection in global markets
- Handling international contracts and disputes

4.6 Human Resources and Talent Management

Managing a global workforce is complex. This section addresses:

- Hiring and retaining talent in different cultures
    - Cultural diversity and inclusion in the workplace
    - Training and development for global teams

4.7 Managing Risk and Uncertainty

Global business is inherently risky, and this section provides insights into:

- Strategies for managing financial and operational risks
    - Scenario planning for uncertainty and crisis management
    - The importance of adaptability in global business

4.8 Case Studies and Practical Insights

Throughout the chapter, real-world case studies and expert interviews provide practical insights into the challenges and successes of global market entry and expansion. Examples include companies that effectively adapted their products and marketing strategies for specific regions and successfully managed legal issues in international markets.

4.9 Conclusion

Chapter 4 highlights the crucial operational and strategic aspects of entering and expanding in global markets. It underscores the importance of adaptability, market customization, and risk management. Entrepreneurs who master the art of execution and growth strategies are better equipped to thrive in the dynamic and diverse international business landscape. This chapter prepares the reader for the subsequent discussion on international marketing and the development of a global brand.

5

International Marketing and Global Brand Development

Introduction

Chapter 5 explores the intricacies of international marketing and the development of a global brand. In a world where global competition is fierce, understanding how to effectively promote products or services across diverse markets and cultures is essential for success. This chapter delves into the strategies, tactics, and best practices of international marketing.

5.1 The Global Marketing Landscape

This section provides an overview of the evolving global marketing landscape. Key points include:

- The impact of cultural diversity on marketing
    - Market-specific consumer behavior and preferences
    - The role of digital technology in international marketing

5.2 Market Research for International Marketing

Before crafting an international marketing strategy, thorough market research is crucial. This part of the chapter covers:

- Conducting cultural, social, and economic research
    - Utilizing insights from local partners and experts
    - Adapting marketing strategies based on market analysis

5.3 Crafting an International Marketing Strategy

Developing a comprehensive marketing strategy for global markets is the focus of this section. It includes:

- Setting global marketing objectives and goals
    - Tailoring marketing messages and content for different markets
    - Choosing the right marketing channels for global outreach

5.4 Global Brand Development

Creating and nurturing a global brand is pivotal for international success. This part of the chapter addresses:

- The importance of brand consistency and integrity
    - Case studies of successful global brands
    - Building brand loyalty in diverse markets

5.5 Cross-Cultural Communication and Localization

Effective communication in global marketing requires understanding cultural nuances. This section discusses:

- The challenges of cross-cultural marketing

- Strategies for localization and adaptation
- Avoiding cultural pitfalls and miscommunication

5.6 Social Media and Digital Marketing in Global Promotion

Digital marketing is a cornerstone of international marketing. This part of the chapter covers:

- Leveraging social media for global brand promotion
    - E-commerce and international online sales
    - Measuring the effectiveness of digital marketing campaigns

5.7 Global Advertising and Promotion

Creating compelling advertisements that resonate with diverse audiences is essential. This section addresses:

- Choosing the right advertising channels for different markets
    - Successful global advertising campaigns
    - The role of storytelling in international advertising

5.8 Measuring Success and Adjusting Strategies

Evaluating the effectiveness of international marketing efforts is critical. This part of the chapter includes:

- Key performance indicators for global marketing campaigns
    - The importance of customer feedback and market data
    - Adjusting marketing strategies based on performance metrics

5.9 Case Studies and Practical Insights

Throughout the chapter, real-world case studies and expert interviews

provide practical insights into successful international marketing strategies and brand development. Examples include companies that effectively localized their marketing campaigns for various regions and built strong global brand identities.

5.10 Conclusion

Chapter 5 underscores the importance of effective international marketing and global brand development. It emphasizes the need for cultural sensitivity, adaptability, and consistent brand messaging across diverse markets. Entrepreneurs who master the art of international marketing are better equipped to build strong global brands and succeed in the competitive world of global business. This chapter paves the way for further discussions on sales and customer service in international markets.

6

Global Sales and Customer Service Excellence

Introduction

Chapter 6 explores the critical aspects of global sales and customer service in the 21st-century business landscape. In a world where customers are diverse and expect high-quality service, mastering the art of international sales and providing exceptional customer service is key to achieving sustained success in global markets.

6.1 The Global Customer-Centric Approach

This section introduces the customer-centric approach and its importance in international sales and customer service. Key points include:

- Understanding diverse customer needs and preferences
    - The impact of cultural factors on customer behavior
    - The role of customer satisfaction in long-term success

6.2 Building a Global Sales Team

A skilled sales team is essential for global success. This part of the chapter addresses:

- Recruiting and training sales professionals for global markets
    - Creating a diverse and adaptable sales force
    - Sales leadership and management strategies

6.3 International Sales Strategies

Developing effective sales strategies for global markets is pivotal. This section covers:

- Identifying global sales channels and markets
    - Pricing and negotiation strategies in international sales
    - Key account management and relationship-building

6.4 Sales Forecasting and Performance Metrics

Measuring sales performance and forecasting are vital for business growth. This part of the chapter discusses:

- Key performance indicators (KPIs) in international sales
    - Data analytics and predictive modeling
    - Adjusting sales strategies based on performance metrics

6.5 Exceptional Customer Service in Global Markets

Providing exceptional customer service is a competitive advantage. This section addresses:

- Cultural sensitivity and diverse customer service approaches

- Multilingual and multi-channel customer support
- Handling customer complaints and issues effectively

6.6 Building Customer Loyalty

Creating and nurturing customer loyalty is crucial in global markets. This part of the chapter discusses:

- Reward and loyalty programs for international customers
    - Case studies of businesses with strong global customer loyalty
    - The role of ongoing communication and engagement

6.7 Cultural Sensitivity and Cross-Cultural Communication

Effective cross-cultural communication is essential in customer service. This section covers:

- The challenges of communicating with diverse customers
    - Strategies for improving cultural sensitivity in customer interactions
    - Avoiding cultural misunderstandings and conflicts

6.8 Technology in Sales and Customer Service

Leveraging technology is pivotal in modern global sales and customer service. This part of the chapter addresses:

- The role of customer relationship management (CRM) systems
    - Chatbots, AI, and automation in customer service
    - Security and data protection in global customer interactions

6.9 Case Studies and Practical Insights

Throughout the chapter, real-world case studies and expert interviews

provide practical insights into successful global sales and customer service strategies. Examples include companies that effectively adapted their sales approaches for different international markets and built strong global customer relationships.

6.10 Conclusion

Chapter 6 underscores the importance of global sales and customer service excellence in achieving sustained success in international markets. It emphasizes the need for cultural sensitivity, a customer-centric approach, and the use of technology to enhance customer interactions. Entrepreneurs who master the art of global sales and exceptional customer service are better equipped to thrive in the competitive global business landscape. This chapter sets the stage for further discussions on global operations and supply chain management.

7

Global Operations and Supply Chain Management

Introduction

Chapter 7 explores the intricacies of global operations and supply chain management in the 21st-century business landscape. Effective management of operations and supply chains is essential for delivering products and services to international customers efficiently and cost-effectively.

7.1 The Complex World of Global Operations

This section provides an overview of global operations and the complexity involved. Key points include:

- Challenges in coordinating operations across borders
  - The importance of efficiency and cost control
  - The role of technology in global operations

7.2 Global Supply Chain Management

Effective supply chain management is crucial for global success. This part of the chapter addresses:

- Managing a global supply chain network
    - Inventory management and demand forecasting
    - Supplier selection and relationship management

7.3 Logistics and Distribution

Efficient logistics and distribution are key to meeting customer demands. This section covers:

- International shipping and transportation methods
    - Warehousing and inventory control
    - Last-mile delivery in global markets

7.4 Lean and Agile Supply Chains

Adopting lean and agile supply chain strategies is increasingly important. This part of the chapter discusses:

- Reducing waste and increasing efficiency in supply chains
    - The role of adaptability in responding to market changes
    - Case studies of successful lean and agile supply chains

7.5 Sustainability and Ethical Considerations

Sustainability and ethics are integral to global operations and supply chain management. This section addresses:

- Environmental sustainability in supply chain operations

- Ethical considerations in supplier relationships
  - Case studies of businesses with sustainable and ethical supply chains

7.6 Risk Management in Global Operations

Managing risks in global operations is essential. This part of the chapter discusses:

- Identifying and assessing operational risks
    - Strategies for risk mitigation and contingency planning
    - Crisis management and business continuity

7.7 Technology and Innovation in Operations

Leveraging technology and innovation is pivotal in modern global operations. This section covers:

- The role of automation and data analytics
    - IoT and real-time monitoring in supply chains
    - Technology adoption for process improvement

7.8 Compliance and Regulatory Challenges

Adhering to international regulations and compliance standards is essential. This part of the chapter addresses:

- Legal considerations in global operations
    - Customs and trade compliance
    - Handling regulatory changes and challenges

7.9 Case Studies and Practical Insights

Throughout the chapter, real-world case studies and expert interviews

provide practical insights into successful global operations and supply chain management strategies. Examples include companies that effectively optimized their supply chains, adopted sustainable practices, and responded to operational crises.

7.10 Conclusion

Chapter 7 underscores the importance of global operations and supply chain management in delivering products and services to international customers efficiently and cost-effectively. It emphasizes the need for adaptability, sustainability, and a deep understanding of global regulations. Entrepreneurs who master the art of global operations and supply chain management are better equipped to thrive in the competitive global business landscape. This chapter sets the stage for further discussions on finance and international expansion strategies.

8

Global Finance and International Expansion Strategies

Introduction

Chapter 8 explores the critical aspects of global finance and international expansion strategies. In a world where capital is essential for growth and expansion, understanding financial strategies and approaches for global business is vital for entrepreneurs and business leaders.

8.1 The Global Financial Landscape

This section provides an overview of the evolving global financial landscape. Key points include:

- The impact of currency fluctuations and exchange rates
    - International financial markets and investments
    - The role of financial technology (fintech) in global finance

8.2 Funding International Expansion

Financing international expansion is a crucial step. This part of the chapter addresses:

- Sources of capital for global expansion
    - Debt financing and equity investment
    - Case studies of companies that successfully financed their international expansion

8.3 Financial Risk Management

Managing financial risks in global operations is pivotal. This section covers:

- Strategies for mitigating currency exchange rate risks
    - Hedging and risk insurance
    - Financial planning for economic and political uncertainties

8.4 Budgeting and Financial Forecasting

Effective financial planning is essential for international expansion. This part of the chapter discusses:

- Creating international budgets
    - Forecasting and managing cash flow
    - Investment analysis and return on investment (ROI)

8.5 Taxation and Compliance

Navigating international taxation and compliance is essential. This section addresses:

- Tax implications of global operations
    - Transfer pricing and cross-border tax strategies
    - International compliance and reporting requirements

8.6 Financial Performance Measurement

Measuring financial performance and success in global business is critical. This part of the chapter includes:

- Key financial performance indicators (KPIs) for global operations
    - Financial reports and dashboards for international businesses
    - Adapting financial strategies based on performance metrics

8.7 Mergers, Acquisitions, and Joint Ventures

Exploring strategic growth through mergers, acquisitions, and joint ventures is essential. This section discusses:

- Identifying potential partners and targets for growth
    - Due diligence in international transactions
    - Post-acquisition integration and management

8.8 International Expansion Strategies

Developing effective international expansion strategies is the focus of this section. It includes:

- Market entry approaches and targeting new regions
    - Diversification and product expansion
    - Scaling up and managing growth in global markets

8.9 Case Studies and Practical Insights

Throughout the chapter, real-world case studies and expert interviews provide practical insights into successful global finance and international expansion strategies. Examples include companies that effectively managed their international finances, leveraged acquisitions for growth, and expanded into new markets.

8.10 Conclusion

Chapter 8 underscores the importance of global finance and international expansion strategies in achieving growth and success in the international business landscape. It emphasizes the need for financial planning, risk management, and adaptability to changing market conditions. Entrepreneurs who master the art of global finance and strategic expansion are better equipped to thrive in the competitive world of global business. This chapter sets the stage for further discussions on innovation and sustainability in the global marketplace.

9

Innovation and Sustainability in the Global Marketplace

Introduction

Chapter 9 explores the critical role of innovation and sustainability in the dynamic global business landscape of the 21st century. To thrive in international markets, businesses must continually innovate and embrace sustainability practices that align with environmental and social responsibilities.

9.1 The Imperative of Innovation

This section highlights the importance of innovation in global business. Key points include:

- The role of innovation in gaining a competitive edge
    - Encouraging a culture of innovation in the organization
    - Leveraging technology and research and development for innovation

9.2 Innovation Strategies for Global Success

Innovating effectively on a global scale requires well-defined strategies. This part of the chapter addresses:

- Open innovation and collaboration with global partners
    - The development of new products and services for international markets
    - Adapting innovation strategies to different cultural and market contexts

9.3 Sustainability and Corporate Social Responsibility (CSR)

Sustainability and CSR are integral to global business operations. This section discusses:

- Sustainable supply chain practices and green initiatives
    - Social responsibility in global operations
    - The impact of sustainability on brand reputation and consumer preferences

9.4 Sustainable Supply Chain Management

Sustainability in supply chain management is pivotal for responsible global business. This part of the chapter covers:

- Reducing environmental impact in supply chain operations
    - Ethical sourcing and fair labor practices
    - Case studies of companies with sustainable supply chains

9.5 Green Marketing and Eco-Friendly Products

Promoting sustainability through green marketing is essential. This section addresses:

- Marketing eco-friendly products in global markets
    - The role of certifications and labeling in green marketing
    - Successful campaigns and consumer engagement in sustainability efforts

9.6 Technological Advancements and Sustainability

Leveraging technology for sustainability is increasingly important. This part of the chapter discusses:

- The role of renewable energy and clean technologies in global operations
    - The use of data analytics and IoT for sustainability efforts
    - Innovation in reducing environmental footprints

9.7 Social Responsibility and Community Engagement

Engaging with local communities and being socially responsible is part of global business. This section covers:

- Community development and engagement programs
    - Philanthropy and corporate social responsibility initiatives
    - Case studies of businesses with successful community engagement efforts

9.8 Innovation and Sustainability Reporting

Transparency in reporting innovation and sustainability efforts is essential. This part of the chapter includes:

- Sustainability reports and corporate disclosures
    - Communicating innovation milestones and achievements
    - Responding to feedback and improving innovation and sustainability strategies

9.9 Case Studies and Practical Insights

Throughout the chapter, real-world case studies and expert interviews provide practical insights into successful innovation and sustainability practices. Examples include companies that effectively integrated sustainability into their business models, achieved innovation breakthroughs, and enhanced their global brand through responsible practices.

9.10 Conclusion

Chapter 9 underscores the importance of innovation and sustainability in the global marketplace. It emphasizes the need for innovation-driven growth and environmentally and socially responsible practices. Entrepreneurs who master the art of innovation and sustainability are better equipped to thrive in the competitive and socially conscious world of global business. This chapter sets the stage for the final chapter, which provides a forward-looking perspective on the future of global business.

10

The Future of Global Business: Trends and Projections

Introduction

Chapter 10 explores the future of global business, identifying emerging trends, challenges, and opportunities that will shape the landscape in the years to come. As the world continues to evolve, businesses must adapt and innovate to thrive in an ever-changing global marketplace.

10.1 Globalization in the Digital Age

This section examines how digital technology is reshaping globalization. Key points include:

- The role of digital platforms and e-commerce in global trade
 - The impact of blockchain and digital currencies on cross-border transactions
 - Strategies for navigating the digital global marketplace

10.2 The Evolving Geopolitical Landscape

The geopolitical landscape continues to impact global business. This part of the chapter addresses:

- The role of political shifts, trade agreements, and sanctions
    - Navigating geopolitical risks and opportunities
    - Case studies of businesses that successfully adapted to geopolitical changes

10.3 Sustainability and ESG (Environmental, Social, and Governance) Factors

Sustainability and ESG considerations are gaining prominence. This section discusses:

- The influence of sustainability and ESG on investment decisions
    - Measuring and reporting ESG performance
    - Strategies for integrating sustainability into global business models

10.4 Artificial Intelligence and Automation

AI and automation are transforming various aspects of global business. This part of the chapter covers:

- The impact of AI on supply chain management, customer service, and decision-making
    - Challenges and opportunities of automation in international operations
    - Preparing for the AI-driven future of global business

10.5 Workforce Transformation

The workforce is evolving, and businesses must adapt to changing employee expectations and demographics. This section addresses:

- Remote work and global talent sourcing
    - The role of diversity and inclusion in the global workforce
    - Strategies for building a resilient and adaptable workforce

10.6 Trade and Environmental Regulations

Environmental regulations are becoming more stringent, impacting international trade. This part of the chapter discusses:

- Green trade policies and carbon tariffs
    - The circular economy and sustainable production
    - Strategies for compliance and innovation in a changing regulatory environment

10.7 Emerging Markets and Growth Opportunities

The chapter explores emerging markets and the potential for international growth. This section covers:

- Identifying and capitalizing on opportunities in emerging markets
    - Managing risks and uncertainties in market expansion
    - Case studies of companies that successfully expanded into emerging markets

10.8 Cybersecurity and Data Privacy

The digital age brings new challenges related to cybersecurity and data privacy. This part of the chapter addresses:

- Protecting sensitive data and customer privacy in international operations
    - Preparing for cybersecurity threats and data breaches
    - Regulatory compliance and global data protection laws

10.9 Forward-Looking Strategies

As the global business landscape evolves, businesses must adopt forward-looking strategies. This section discusses:

- The importance of scenario planning and adaptability
    - Innovations in business models and strategies
    - Preparing for the future with agility and resilience

10.10 Conclusion

Chapter 10 provides a forward-looking perspective on the future of global business. It emphasizes the need for adaptability, innovation, and a deep understanding of emerging trends and challenges. Entrepreneurs and business leaders who prepare for the future are better equipped to thrive in the dynamic and ever-evolving global marketplace. This chapter serves as a closing reflection on the evolving nature of global business and the constant need for strategic thinking and adaptation.

11

Strategic Leadership in Global Business

Introduction

Chapter 11 delves into the role of strategic leadership in the dynamic world of global business. Effective leadership is pivotal in navigating the complex global landscape, implementing strategies, and fostering innovation. This chapter explores the traits, skills, and practices of leaders in international business.

11.1 The Role of Leadership in Global Business

This section highlights the importance of leadership in the global business context. Key points include:

- The impact of leadership on organizational culture and success
    - The challenges and complexities of leading international teams
    - The need for adaptable and visionary leaders

11.2 Traits and Characteristics of Effective Global Leaders

Effective global leaders possess distinct traits and characteristics. This part of the chapter addresses:

- Traits such as adaptability, cultural sensitivity, and emotional intelligence
    - The role of vision and strategic thinking in global leadership
    - Building a global leadership team with diverse skills and backgrounds

11.3 Leading Diverse and Cross-Cultural Teams

Global business often involves diverse and cross-cultural teams. This section discusses:

- Strategies for effective cross-cultural leadership and communication
    - Team-building and fostering collaboration in international contexts
    - Case studies of successful cross-cultural leadership

11.4 Leading Innovation and Change

Innovation and change are integral to global business success. This part of the chapter covers:

- Leading innovation through a culture of experimentation and learning
    - Strategies for embracing change and navigating disruption
    - Encouraging and managing innovative teams

11.5 Ethical Leadership and Corporate Responsibility

Ethical leadership and corporate responsibility are paramount in global business. This section addresses:

- Leading with integrity and ethical decision-making
    - Incorporating corporate social responsibility into leadership practices
    - Case studies of ethical leadership and responsible business practices

11.6 Crisis Leadership and Risk Management

Crisis leadership and risk management are essential in global business. This part of the chapter discusses:

- Crisis response strategies and crisis communication
    - Preparing for and managing global business risks
    - Case studies of leaders who effectively handled crises

11.7 Strategic Decision-Making and Planning

Strategic decision-making and planning are core leadership functions. This section covers:

- Effective strategic planning and execution
    - The role of data-driven decision-making in global business
    - Strategies for alignment and execution of global business strategies

11.8 Mentoring and Talent Development

Mentoring and talent development are crucial for leadership success. This part of the chapter addresses:

- The importance of leadership development programs
    - Strategies for mentoring and nurturing future leaders
    - Building a talent pipeline for global business expansion

11.9 Leadership in a Digital World

The digital age brings new challenges for leadership. This section discusses:

- The impact of digital technology on leadership practices
    - Leading remote and virtual teams

- Developing a digital-savvy leadership team

11.10 Conclusion

Chapter 11 emphasizes the critical role of strategic leadership in global business. It underscores the need for adaptable, ethical, and visionary leaders who can navigate the complexities of international markets. Entrepreneurs and business leaders who embrace effective leadership practices are better equipped to succeed in the dynamic and interconnected world of global business. This chapter serves as a reflection on the importance of leadership in shaping the future of global business.

12

Global Business Ethics and Responsible Citizenship

Introduction

Chapter 12 delves into the importance of business ethics and responsible citizenship in the global business landscape. In an interconnected world, businesses are expected to operate with integrity and contribute positively to society. This chapter explores the ethical principles and practices that guide responsible global business conduct.

12.1 The Role of Ethics in Global Business

This section highlights the fundamental role of ethics in global business. Key points include:

- The impact of ethical business practices on reputation and customer trust
    - The challenges and complexities of ethical decision-making in international contexts
        - The need for a strong ethical foundation in global organizations

12.2 Core Principles of Global Business Ethics

Global business ethics are guided by core principles. This part of the chapter addresses:

- Ethical principles such as honesty, transparency, and fairness
    - Legal and regulatory compliance in global operations
    - The role of corporate codes of conduct and ethics committees

12.3 Ethical Challenges in International Markets

Operating in international markets presents specific ethical challenges. This section discusses:

- Navigating cultural differences and ethical relativism
    - Ethical dilemmas related to bribery, corruption, and labor practices
    - Strategies for addressing ethical challenges in global business

12.4 Corporate Social Responsibility (CSR)

Corporate social responsibility is integral to global business ethics. This part of the chapter covers:

- CSR initiatives, philanthropy, and community engagement
    - Environmental sustainability and responsible business practices
    - Case studies of businesses with successful CSR programs

12.5 Human Rights and Labor Practices

Respecting human rights and fair labor practices is a key ethical consideration. This section addresses:

- Ensuring fair labor conditions and worker rights in global operations

- Ethical supply chain management and responsible sourcing
- Case studies of businesses that prioritize human rights and labor standards

12.6 Environmental Stewardship

Environmental stewardship is a growing ethical concern. This part of the chapter discusses:

- Reducing environmental impact and promoting sustainable practices
    - Environmental regulations and compliance in global operations
    - Strategies for embedding environmental responsibility in the corporate culture

12.7 Ethical Leadership and Decision-Making

Ethical leadership and decision-making are pivotal in responsible global business. This section covers:

- Leading with integrity and ethical transparency
    - The role of leaders in promoting ethical behavior within organizations
    - Case studies of ethical leaders who have made a positive impact

12.8 Transparency, Reporting, and Accountability

Transparency and accountability are essential components of ethical global business. This part of the chapter includes:

- Ethical reporting and disclosure practices
    - Accountability mechanisms and stakeholder engagement
    - Strategies for building trust through transparency

12.9 Ethical Citizenship and Philanthropy

Responsible citizenship and philanthropy contribute to ethical business conduct. This section addresses:

- Supporting local communities and global causes
  - The role of philanthropy in addressing social issues
  - Case studies of businesses that practice ethical citizenship

12.10 Conclusion

Chapter 12 underscores the significance of global business ethics and responsible citizenship. It emphasizes the need for a strong ethical foundation and the integration of ethical principles into all aspects of global business. Entrepreneurs and business leaders who prioritize ethical conduct are better equipped to thrive in the interconnected and ethically conscious world of global business. This chapter serves as a closing reflection on the importance of responsible business conduct and its impact on the global community.

Chapter 12: Global Business Ethics and Responsible Citizenship

In Chapter 12, the focus is on the pivotal role of business ethics and responsible citizenship in the global business landscape. It highlights the growing importance of operating with integrity and contributing positively to society in an interconnected world. The chapter explores the ethical principles and practices that guide responsible global business conduct.

The chapter begins by emphasizing the fundamental role of ethics in global business. It underscores how ethical practices not only build a positive reputation but also foster customer trust. However, it acknowledges the complex nature of ethical decision-making in international contexts.

Core principles of global business ethics are examined, including honesty, transparency, fairness, and the necessity of adhering to legal and regulatory requirements. Corporate codes of conduct and ethics committees are discussed as tools to promote ethical behavior within organizations.

Operating in international markets poses specific ethical challenges due to cultural differences and ethical relativism. Ethical dilemmas related to bribery, corruption, and labor practices are addressed, and strategies for addressing these challenges are explored.

Corporate Social Responsibility (CSR) is explored as an integral part of global business ethics. The chapter delves into CSR initiatives, philanthropy, community engagement, environmental sustainability, and responsible business practices, with case studies showcasing businesses with successful CSR programs.

The importance of respecting human rights and fair labor practices in global business is highlighted. Ensuring fair labor conditions and worker rights in global operations, along with ethical supply chain management, is discussed with reference to real-world case studies.

Environmental stewardship, another ethical concern, is examined in the context of reducing environmental impact and promoting sustainable practices. The chapter also covers environmental regulations and compliance in global operations.

Ethical leadership and decision-making are seen as pivotal in responsible global business. The role of leaders in promoting ethical behavior within organizations is discussed, along with case studies highlighting the impact of ethical leaders.

Transparency, reporting, and accountability are essential components of ethical global business. Strategies for achieving trust through transparency, ethical reporting, and stakeholder engagement are presented.

The chapter also touches on responsible citizenship and philanthropy, emphasizing the importance of supporting local communities and global causes, with case studies showcasing businesses that practice ethical citizenship.

Chapter 12 concludes by underlining the significance of global business ethics and responsible citizenship. It underscores the need for a strong ethical foundation and the integration of ethical principles into all aspects of global business. Entrepreneurs and business leaders who prioritize ethical conduct are better equipped to thrive in the interconnected and ethically conscious world of global business. This chapter serves as a closing reflection on the importance of responsible business conduct and its impact on the global community.

www.ingramcontent.com/pod-product-compliance
Lightning Source LLC
LaVergne TN
LVHW012129070526
838202LV00056B/5928